WHERE DOES THE GARBAGE GO?

BY PAUL SHOWERS · ILLUSTRATED BY RANDY CHEWNING

Revised Edition

HARPER

An Imprint of HarperCollinsPublishers

Special thanks to Robin Woods of the United States Environmental Protection Agency, William Rathje, founder of the Garbage Project at the University of Arizona, and Thomas Frankiewicz for their expert advice and information.

The illustrations in this book were prepared with Winsor and Newton Brilliant Watercolours and a .35 pen on two-ply Strathmore 500 Bristol paper.

The Let's-Read-and-Find-Out Science book series was originated by Dr. Franklyn M. Branley, Astronomer Emeritus and former Chairman of the American Museum of Natural History–Hayden Planetarium, and was formerly co-edited by him and Dr. Roma Gans, Professor Emeritus of Childhood Education, Teachers College, Columbia University. Text and illustrations for each of the books in the series are checked for accuracy by an expert in the relevant field. For more information about Let's-Read-and-Find-Out Science books, write to HarperCollins Children's Books, 195 Broadway, New York, NY 10007, or visit our website at www.letsreadandfindout.com.

Let's Read-and-Find-Out Science® is a trademark of HarperCollins Publishers.

Library of Congress Cataloging-in-Publication Data
Showers, Paul.
    Where does the garbage go? / by Paul Showers ; illustrated by Randy Chewning. — Rev. ed.
        p.   cm. — (Let's-read-and-find-out science. Stage 2)
    Summary: Explains how people create too much waste and how waste is now recycled and put into landfills.
    ISBN 978-0-06-021057-1 (lib. bdg.) — ISBN 978-0-06-238200-9 (pbk.)
    1. Refuse and refuse disposal—Juvenile literature.   [1. Refuse and refuse disposal. 2. Recycling (Waste)]
I. Chewning, Randy, ill.   II. Title.   III. Series.
TD792.S48   1994   91-46115
628.4'4—dc20   CIP
                                                                                                                AC

17 18 19   SCP   10 9 8 7 6 5

❖

Revised edition, 2015

WHERE DOES THE GARBAGE GO?

In our school we are learning about garbage. Last week our teacher told us about the way things used to be and what we can do to create less garbage and help our environment.

She said there was a time when people who wanted to get rid of something just threw it into the garbage can. They threw away old orange peels, egg shells, and the food they didn't eat. They also threw away things like empty bottles and cans, cardboard boxes, and newspapers.

I would have eaten that.

If kept separate, a lot of food that is thrown away could be turned into compost, which is helpful for growing plants. Old bottles and newspapers could be recycled and made into new materials. But when these things are mixed together, it all becomes garbage.

Once a week the garbage was collected in trucks and taken out to the dump.

In the dump there were piles of garbage everywhere and all kinds of trash—old tires, broken bottles, tin cans, old newspapers, and broken chairs and sofas. In summer the food that was thrown out rotted and made a terrible stink. Rats came to eat it. Millions of flies buzzed around. The dump was a great big mess.

At one time New York City used the ocean for its dump. It loaded its waste on flat boats called barges. Tugboats pulled the barges out to sea, and the waste was dumped overboard. Most of the trash sank, but some of it floated.

ugh!

Often it floated right back to the beaches where people were swimming. *Ugh! Yeccch!*

New York City doesn't throw its waste in the ocean anymore. It has a special kind of dump called a landfill. Other cities have landfills, too. Our town has one, and our class went out and looked at it.

A landfill is a busy place.

Trucks bring loads of waste from the city and dump it in big piles.

Bulldozers with scrapers spread out the waste.

Compactors with spikes on their wheels move back and forth over it. The waste is all mashed and piled.

After that, trucks bring loads of soil. The bulldozers and compactors spread the soil over the waste. The soil covers up everything. It keeps out the rats and flies.

Then the landfill is ready for more waste. Then comes more soil to cover it up—then more waste and more soil, layer after layer. A landfill keeps piling up. It gets to be a little mountain.

The layers of a landfill

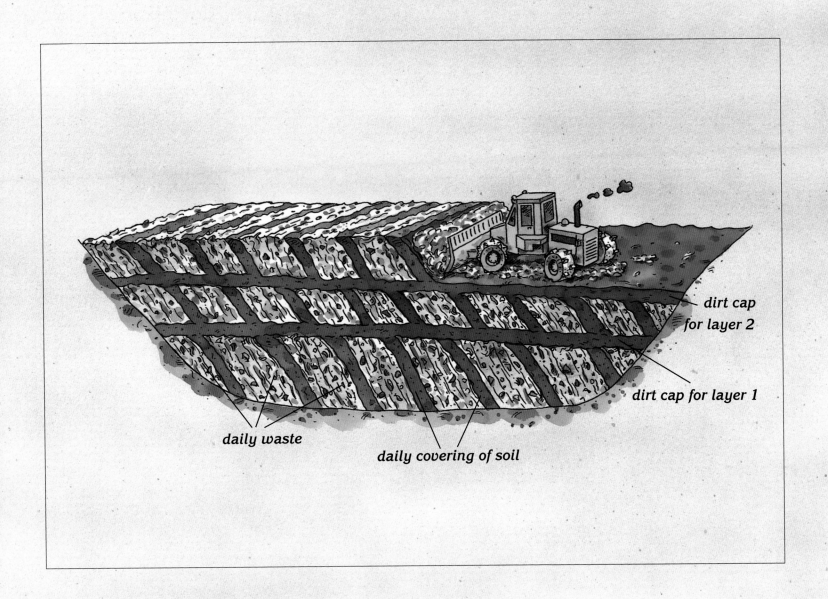

dirt cap for layer 2

dirt cap for layer 1

daily waste

daily covering of soil

When the last layer of soil is spread on top of a landfill, grass and trees are planted on it. The landfill becomes a park or playground.

Then the city has to find a new place to dispose of its garbage. Garbage never stops piling up.

What is in our landfills?

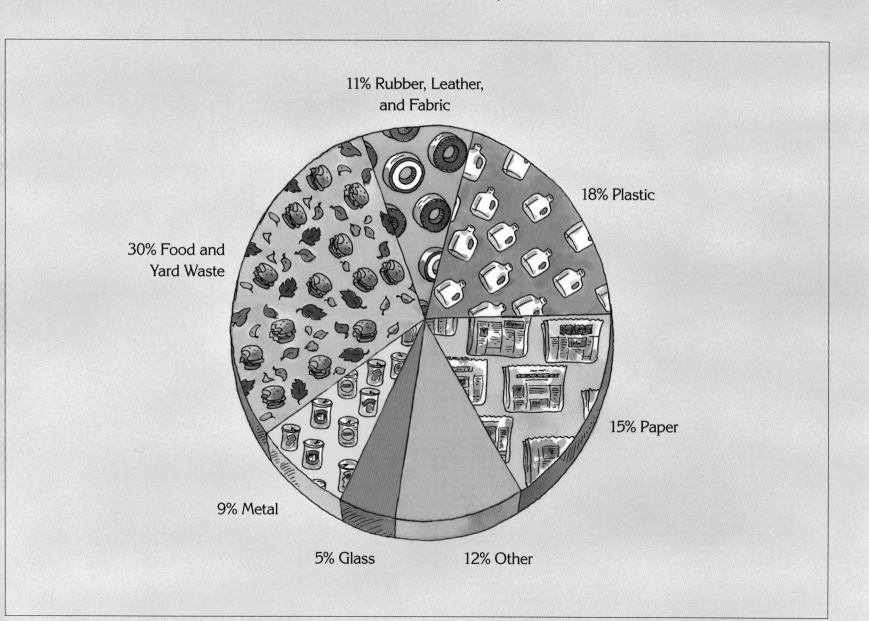

11% Rubber, Leather, and Fabric

18% Plastic

30% Food and Yard Waste

15% Paper

9% Metal

5% Glass

12% Other

Some cities try to get rid of their waste by burning it. They build big furnaces called incinerators and burn garbage and trash in them. The heat is used to warm stores and offices. It is also used to make electricity.

How an incinerator works

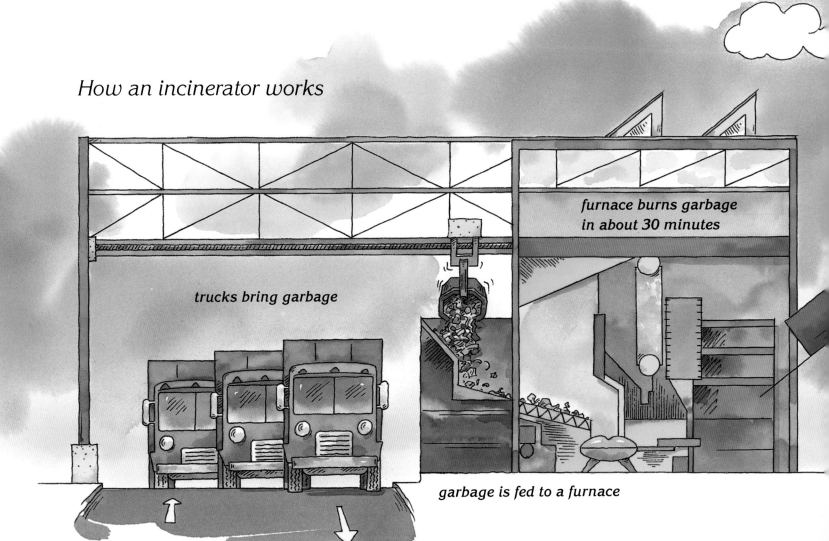

trucks bring garbage

furnace burns garbage in about 30 minutes

garbage is fed to a furnace

When incinerators burn our trash, they don't really get rid of everything. There is leftover ash that still has to go to a landfill. Sometimes this ash is toxic or harmful. And sometimes the smoke from the incinerator pollutes the air with harmful gases.

cleaned gases are released

gases from the burning garbage must be carefully cleaned and filtered

Today cities are having a hard time finding places for new landfills. Waste keeps piling up. People keep throwing things away. They throw away too many things. Some of the things they throw away could be used over again.

Each person in the U.S. creates about four pounds of trash every day.

One way cities make less garbage is by recycling.
Recycling means making trash into something new
instead of throwing it away.

*Almost half
of the trash
we throw away
could be
recycled. Look
for this symbol
on glass, paper,
metal, and plastic
containers that
can be recycled.*

My family tries to recycle as much as it can. We turn old fruits, vegetables, and grass clippings into compost for our yards. We keep garbage like glass bottles, aluminum cans, newspapers, and foil separate from the food waste. When we put the cans and bottles at the curb, we pile old newspapers beside them. We flatten our cardboard boxes and pile them next to the newspapers to be picked up for recycling each week.

When the garbage truck comes, it picks up only the garbage and takes it out to the landfill. Other trucks come for the bottles and cans and newspapers. Those things don't go to the landfill anymore. Our city sells them to factories and mills for recycling.

Paper mills chop up old newspapers and turn them into new paper.

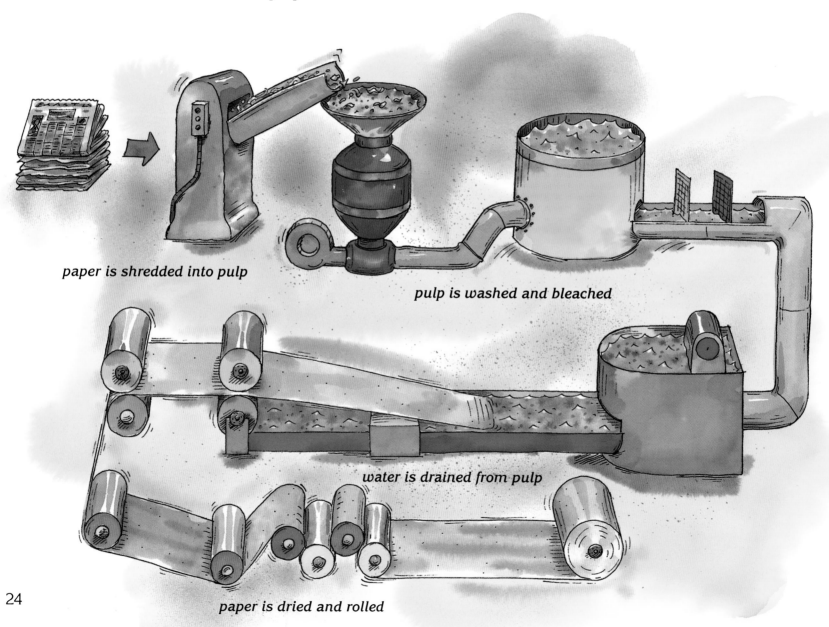

paper is shredded into pulp

pulp is washed and bleached

water is drained from pulp

paper is dried and rolled

Aluminum factories take aluminum cans and foil and melt them to make new cans and rolls of foil.

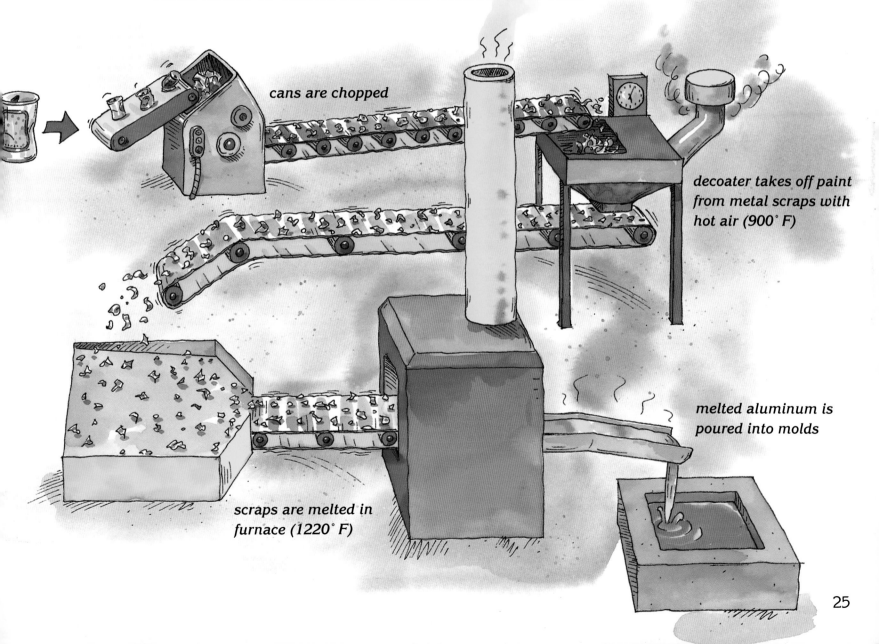

cans are chopped

decoater takes off paint from metal scraps with hot air (900° F)

scraps are melted in furnace (1220° F)

melted aluminum is poured into molds

Glass bottles are ground up and melted to make new glass bottles and jars.

other glass bottles are crushed

glass is melted in a furnace

some bottles are sterilized and reused

blown-in air cools glass

gobs of molten glass are poured into molds

Even plastic can be recycled. Plastic factories chop it up and turn it into things like flowerpots and park benches.

plastic is chopped into bits

bits are washed and dried

plastic is melted and poured into a mold

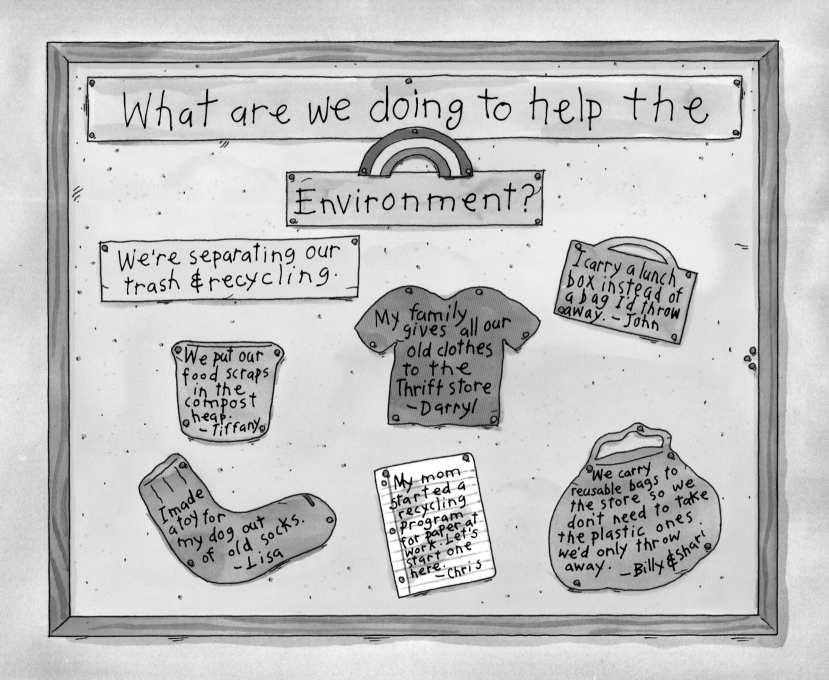

Our teacher says recycling is a good start, but we must do more. We must stop making so much waste. We must stop throwing so many things away. We need to find ways to use things over and over again.

That's what we have done at home. We used to bring our groceries home in paper and plastic bags. When we emptied the bags, we threw them away in the garbage can. When we did that, we were just making more waste to pile up in the landfill.

We have stopped doing that. Now we use reusable bags. They hang on the kitchen doorknob. When we go to the supermarket, we take our reusable bags and put our groceries in them.

Our reusable bags are strong and hold a lot of
groceries. We use them over and over again.